Professional Development for Teachers and Administrators

(A guide)

Written by

Maria Onyia (PhD, Ed)

Published by

Authors Writers

64, Holmes Street, Ile-Iwe B/stop, Behind Synagogue Church,

Ikotun, Lagos

08039251939

CONTENTS

DEDICATION

Dedicated to Prof Chidi Onyia, OrgLearning leaders and teachers around the world.

ACKNOWLEDGEMENT

I express my gratitude to God, the creator of all things, who bestows us the blessing of success in all our endeavours.

A heartfelt thank you goes to Ezeudo na Udo, Prof. Sir Chidiebere Onyia, for your unwavering support and continuous encouragement in my pursuits.

To my beloved biological children, Tobechukwu, Kenechukwu, Ikechukwu, Uchechukwu, and all my cherished adopted children, please know that my love for you knows no bounds.

A special mention is reserved for the remarkable team and family at Orglearning Consult and Academies.

To my dearest family, friends, and colleagues, your presence is a constant source of wonder and joy. Your support and camaraderie mean the world to me.

INTRODUCTION

Structured training is of great importance to school owners, school administrators, and all teachers because teachers play a crucial role in ensuring academic success, character development, skills acquisition and overall educational advancement.

Well-trained teachers possess the knowledge and skills to effectively convey instructions and engage students meaningfully in and outside the classroom. Educators are also able to affect behaviours when they have a deep understanding of how students learn. Their efficacy allows them to provide quality education and ensure students receive the best possible learning experience, leading to the application of learned skills.

Training equips teachers with innovative tutoring methods, the ability to adapt to diverse classroom environments, and the skills needed to improve students' behaviours. Knowledge of teaching methodologies is essential in catering to the unique needs and learning styles of students, fostering a more inclusive and equitable educational environment.

Teacher training emphasizes the importance of continuous development, encourages scholarly research, promotes the use of technology in the classroom, teaches strategies that align with best practices and, at the same time, enhances overall effectiveness in the school.

Structured training empowers teachers to address the social and emotional needs of students, promoting their overall well-being and creating a safe and supportive learning environment. Additionally, trained teachers are better equipped to identify and address learning difficulties or behavioural issues, ensuring early intervention and support for struggling students.

When teachers are trained well, they employ critical thinking, creativity, and problem-solving skills while teaching. Students taught by trained teachers become lifelong learners.

Well-trained teachers also serve as positive role models and a source of inspiration and motivation to students. Students taught by well-trained teachers typically maximize their potential and become the best version of themselves.

For these reasons and others, I have compiled this handbook as a reference for teachers and school owners who wish to see positive transformation in their schools. This handbook is the first of many handbooks to be published and prepared for new and experienced teachers who want to stand out and be seen as masters of the game in a short window.

Enjoy!

Maria R. Onyia (PhD, Ed)

1

CLASSROOM ARRANGEMENT FOR LEARNING

At the beginning of every school year, one of the most important duties of a teacher is to determine the setting of the classroom, particularly the seating arrangement of the learners. Gone are the days when classes were arranged in the traditional pattern where every student faced the teacher, leaving little or no room for student-student interaction. Today, classroom arrangements can take on many varied patterns.

What is Classroom Arrangement?

Classroom arrangement refers to the way furniture, seats, and other learning resources are organised within a classroom to facilitate effective teaching and learning. It includes decisions about the placement of desks, chairs, whiteboards, teachers' desks, and other instructional materials to create an environment conducive to learning. The arrangement can vary depending on the teaching style, grade level, and specific educational goals hoped to be achieved.

The physical configuration of a classroom is an organisational or stylistic choice of the instructor.

However, this configuration could play a major role in the overall mental well-being of a learner. Schools are meant to teach students how to interact, be innovative, and think critically, as well as build their intellect. Thus, a classroom is where learners should pick up the relevance of teamwork and collaboration, and seating arrangement impacts greatly on this.

In-person classroom seating arrangements affect student learning, motivation, participation, and teacher-student and student-student relationships (Fernandez, Huang, & Ronaldo 2011). Student-student relationships are often overlooked, but they are as important as teacher-student relationships. In recent times, the decision to change the traditional classroom arrangement has been made to enhance students' collaboration, engagement, focus, and participation. Research has proven that classroom arrangements can affect the level of communality among students.

There are various teaching methods for diverse lessons to ensure successful delivery by the instructor and retention by the students. Therefore, classroom arrangements should be dictated by the lesson being taught and the teaching method being used by the teacher as well. Some lessons could require that students work in groups or teams, and so seats should be placed in a way to boost teamwork. This might alter the original seating pattern of the class. Other times, there is the need to give a presentation, which also requires a special pattern of arrangement. Every method needs a suitable classroom arrangement. However, for best results, teachers can determine their teaching methods at the beginning of the term and structure their classroom arrangement to fit this pattern.

The next section will explore common classroom arrangements, which include the traditional arrangement, pairs, pods, and others, and how the combination of one or two of these arrangements can support various teaching methods and improve student engagement.

Common Types of Classroom Arrangements

1. **The Traditional Arrangement**: The traditional classroom arrangement is the most common and can be found in many schools. In a typical traditional arrangement, the seats are arranged in rows and columns in such a way that students face the teacher while lessons go on. This classroom seating arrangement restricts student-to-student

communication as it would be difficult to turn backwards to interact with others. In this method, the highest interactions are always between teachers and the students occupying the first rows of the classroom. Students sitting in the back rows are likely to be less engaged.

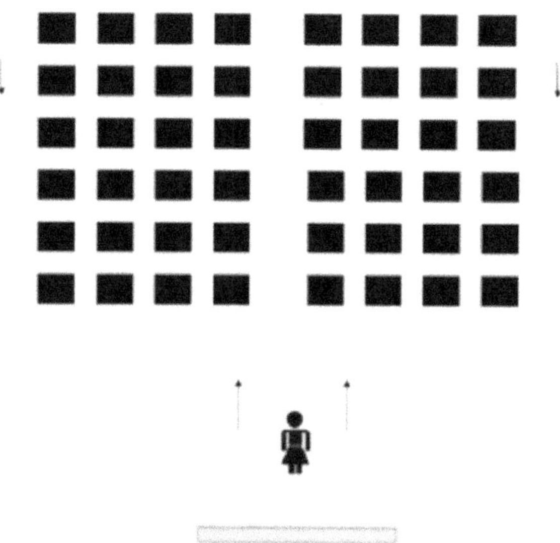

Image Courtesy: Research gate

2. **The Pair Arrangement**: This arrangement is also a very common classroom seating pattern. Students sit in pairs and work individually or in the assigned pair. If they have to work individually, maybe during a test, a binder folder can be placed between the students to guarantee that they work independently.

Pairs allow the teacher to easily divide the classroom into three columns made up of pairs and give them different tasks, assessments, or roles per column or row depending on what is ongoing in the classroom at the time.

Image courtesy: Differentiated teaching

3. **The Roundtable Arrangement**: The most conspicuous example of this is found in seminar-course rooms and office conference rooms during a roundtable discussion. In a classroom setting, students sit around a single large table with the instructor at one end. This seating arrangement can be formed using individual desks. The desks will be

arranged roundly. Students and instructors face one another in this setup. It encourages dialogue among the students as well as the teacher. The teacher can divide his or her attention equally among all students.

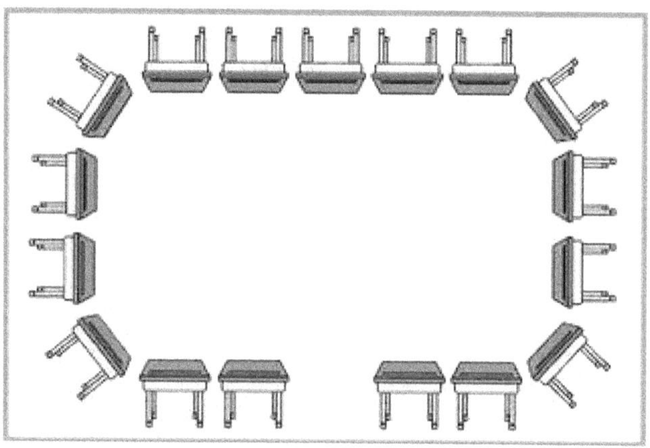

Image courtesy: Fishyrobb.com

4. **The Pod Arrangement** (Groups of Four): If a teacher's aim is for students to collaborate or work in teams, then the class should be arranged in small groups of four, which is also known as the pod arrangement. This seating arrangement works for both individual and group learning. It gives the classroom an interactive or social air as students in each pod can get to know each other better and become friends. This seating arrangement, although not common, is a great one that should be encouraged in schools. The arrangement can be set

up with rectangular, circular, or trapezoidal tables or individual desks. On the whole, this arrangement fosters a learning community where students work with one another.

Image courtesy: ESL Authority

5. Computer Combination: Any of the classroom arrangements can work with portable computers such as laptops, Chromebooks, or tablets. However, the semi-circle or U shape works best for this, as it enables the instructor to easily supervise how the students use the computer to avoid wrong use.

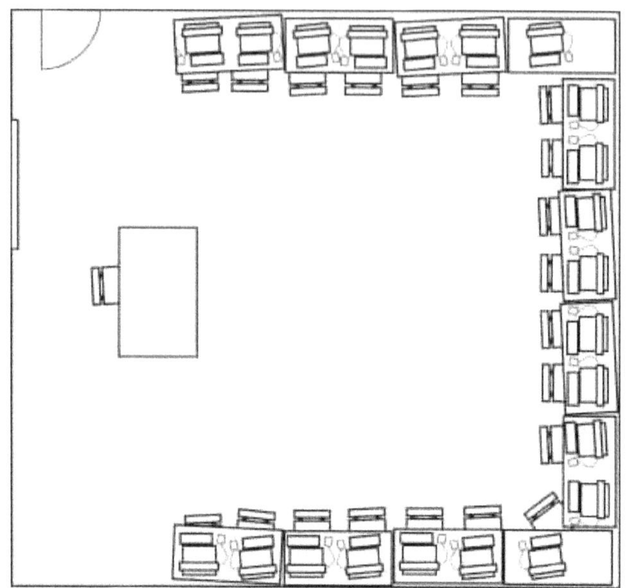

Image courtesy: Helpfulprofessor.com

6. **U-shape, Horseshoe, or Semicircle Arrangement**: If an instructor wants to encourage independent learning, then the U-shape classroom arrangement is perfect because it encourages the students to focus on the teacher and makes it easy for the teacher to observe students and give one-on-one help. However, this arrangement is detrimental to group activity. It discourages student interaction. This setup tends to increase engagement between the instructor and students and between students who sit directly opposite each other, but the distance does not leave much room for proper cooperation.

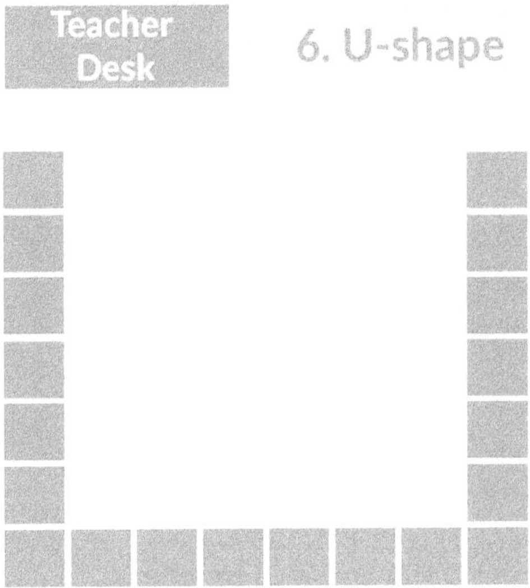

Image courtesy: Book Widgets

7. **Table Groups**: Table groups of four, or as determined by the teacher, can be formed as a part of the classroom behaviour management plan. Table groups are a great way to inspire team spirit among students in the same group and facilitate friendly competitions among the different groups. As a verified method, it is great for encouraging on-task behaviour.

GROUPS/TEAMS

Image courtesy: Differentiated teaching

2

MONITORING LEARNING PROGRESS

Tracking learning progress is very important and should be one of the core responsibilities of every teacher. There are various means through which teachers monitor and assess students' performance. These different methods could be used independently or combined, depending on the observations of the teacher and what he or she hopes to achieve.

Monitoring the learning progress of students entails the regular assessment and tracking of students' academic development, skill acquisition, and understanding of the subjects taught. The monitoring process often includes, but is not limited to, tests, quizzes, examinations, assignments, and observations. The performance of the students enables educators to identify strengths, weaknesses, and areas that need additional support, which helps them modify their instructions and teaching methods to meet the individual needs of the students.

Monitoring enables:

- The teacher to understand how the students interpret learning.
- The students to receive feedback that can enhance their learning.

- The teacher to address the gaps in understanding and develop efficacious teaching methods.

Importance of Student Monitoring

Here are some of the benefits of monitoring student learning.

1. **Aids the discovery of learning challenges and improvements**

   Educators can easily identify the learning challenges of students based on their performance. This knowledge will enable educators to adjust or even change their methods to address the issues that may have arisen. Monitoring also points out to teachers when a student has improved in a particular area or subject. It helps guide educators in deciding whether or not they need to spend more time on a particular topic with the entire class.

2. **Delivers personalised instructions**

   Class monitoring bestows on teachers the knowledge of the effectiveness of their teaching methods, which will, in turn, help them adapt their methods to match different learning styles and patterns. This will make certain that all learners have a chance to grasp what they are taught, in line with their strengths. Teachers will be able to issue personalised instructions or corrections on ways to improve if proper monitoring is done. It helps determine if educators need to give more attention to certain students.

3. **Assists parents**

   Some parents do not know their children's best learning methods and techniques. However, student monitoring provides educators with the necessary data to update parents on their children's academic achievements, areas of weakness, and areas needing improvement. Parents can use this information to play their part in ensuring that the child makes an effort to improve in weak areas. The teacher can also share tips on how parents can teach their children at home based on their children's unique learning styles.

4. **Motivates students**

   Over the years, it has been proven that when attention is paid to students individually and regular feedback and monitoring are provided, they tend to improve their performance, and this is what student monitoring can help achieve. When students know they are being observed, they are more likely to stay engaged and put in more effort. They are motivated to do better because they are aware that they are being monitored.

5. **Promotes accountability**

Overall, monitoring students learning progress promotes accountability in the school because the findings from the report help to know which teachers are assets to their classes. Progress reports do not lie. The school will be able to identify teachers who are putting in the work to adapt to the different needs of the students. Monitoring students' learning progress enables educators to be more productive and adaptable in utilising their teaching methods, leading to an improved learning outcome for the student.

How to Guide and Monitor Student Learning

Despite the various methods for guiding and monitoring student learning, teachers and educators often encounter challenges during the monitoring process. There are various strategies and tools to combat these challenges and ensure that teachers properly track students' progress and engage them satisfactorily using prescribed learning resources. As straightforward as this approach appears, it is not as clear-cut. To make it easier for educators, here are certain methodologies they can imbibe.

- **Identify learning objectives**

Before the beginning of a lesson, educators need to identify three imperative elements: what will be taught, how the lesson will be delivered, and the measures that will be used to determine if students have truly learned. After defining these objectives for the lesson, the teacher should explain them to the class so each student will know what is required of them.

- **Use different teaching methods**
  Different teaching methods such as group discussions, direct lectures, outdoor activities, and hands-on projects should be incorporated to adapt to students' different learning styles. Also, student participation should be encouraged by getting them to be actively involved in discussing the topic, asking questions, and sharing their thoughts.

- **Assess frequently**
  Formative assessment methods like quizzes, polls, and assignments can be employed to gauge each student's understanding of the textbooks and other learning materials. Then, it becomes easier to adjust the teaching approach based on the results.

- **Provide feedback**
  Educators should provide students with constructive feedback on assignments and assessments at

intervals. This feedback should also highlight their strengths, weaknesses, and areas where they have improved and still need to improve.

- **Adjust teaching methods**
Teaching methods should be dynamic rather than static; hence, there should be a continuous assessment of the efficacy of the teaching methods and alter them based on findings and outcomes.

Phases of Student Learning Monitoring

The purpose of student learning monitoring is to create an environment where students feel supported, engaged, and motivated to bring out their best. Therefore, by consistently guiding, monitoring, and tailoring teaching methods to suit their strengths and address their weaknesses, teachers can help ensure that each student's learning needs are met. There are three phases of student learning monitoring. Like scientific findings, monitoring a student's learning progress should be done in stages. These stages are at the beginning, middle, and end of a lesson for proper evaluation.

Student Learning Monitoring at the Beginning of the Lesson

"If you can't explain it simply, you don't understand it well enough."

- **Albert Einstein**

This phase comprises steps to take at the beginning of each lesson to track students' learning progress. To monitor students' progress at the beginning of the lesson, here are some techniques to employ:

1. **Ask questions**

   Before the commencement of each lesson, teachers can ask the students questions on the topic to determine their level of prior knowledge of the subject. Their responses will help the teachers determine what the students already know, what they do not know, and what to consolidate or change.

2. **Give entry slips or entrance tickets**

   Some educators call this "daily work" or "board work". Before the commencement of the day's lesson, teachers can provide students with review questions to answer to demonstrate their understanding of previously taught materials. However, quick feedback should be given on these tickets.

3. **Grade out loudly**

   When grading the whole class' homework from the previous lesson, teachers can call out each person's score. This will motivate students to take their assignments seriously.

4. **Make adjustments**

    If it turns out that, over time, most students still do not understand previously taught lessons, teachers may have to review their teaching methods before moving on. If most of the students are struggling, the teaching methods should be adjusted. However, if only a few students have this problem, they should be given a bit more focus as the lesson goes on.

Student Learning Monitoring During the Lesson

"If a child can't learn the way we teach, maybe we should teach the way they learn."

-   **Ignacio Estrada**

When the lesson is ongoing, there are some methods educators can use to monitor students' progress. Here are some of them:

1. **Eye contact**

    When teachers focus more on just a section of the class, the rest of the class tends to lose interest since they assume they are not being watched, but eye contact from the teachers can correct this notion and get them to be more attentive. The teacher's eyes should move around the room and observe students' countenance, posture, and behaviour to know which one is confused, lost, or distracted and get them to focus.

2. **Reassurance**

   While teaching, teachers should ask the students at intervals if they comprehend the lesson. Teachers should reassure the students that if they do not understand it, they (the teachers) are willing to take it again to enable them to understand it better.

3. **Intermittent questions**

   Students should be randomly asked questions on the topic being taught. It helps to check their understanding and also provides them with the motivation to pay attention because they could be asked impromptu questions.

4. **Adjustments**

   If most of the students being asked questions appear not to have a firm comprehension of the lesson, the teacher might just need to adjust the methods right there and then.

Student Learning Monitoring at the End of the Lesson

"Without continual growth and progress, such words as improvement, achievement, and success have no meaning."

- **Benjamin Franklin**

When the lesson is over, there are ways educators can assess their students to help them better prepare for the next lesson. Here are some methods:

1. **Classwork**

Immediately after a lesson, teachers can engage their students in a quick classwork where they ask their students questions about the just concluded lesson. The students will be graded immediately after the class and their reports submitted to them. This helps educators assess if their teaching methods were suitable and had a positive impact on the majority of the students.

2. **Homework**

Students should be given homework at the end of the day on each topic so they can have time to reflect and study the topics themselves. Some students only need to spend time on the subject themselves for better understanding. Homeworks should be given regularly and should be based on the topics taught that day.

3. **Test**

Tests are similar to classwork but different. Most times, classwork is graded but not recorded, whereas tests are graded and recorded as part of the term's continuous assessment results. If tests are administered, graded regularly, and returned with feedback, students can measure their performance and improve significantly.

3
CLASSROOM MANAGEMENT

At the beginning of every session, teachers should pay great attention to classroom management because an improperly managed class will only produce poorly managed students. Consequently, schools and teachers must ensure classroom management is properly handled daily. Workshops should be held to teach teachers how to manage their classes. Books such as this will also be of great help.

What is Classroom Management?

Classroom management refers to the strategies, techniques, and skills teachers employ to create a productive and orderly learning environment within a classroom. It is the process of ensuring that classroom lessons run smoothly without disorderly behavioural dispositions from students compromising the delivery of instruction through maintaining discipline, fostering student engagement, promoting positive behaviour, and optimising teaching conditions.

Although the concept of classroom management seems straightforward, it is a difficult aspect of teaching for many teachers. In a nutshell, classroom management entails:

- Building a respectable relationship with students.
- Being prepared for classes.
- Establishing behavioural standards that promote students learning.
- Providing a safe and comfortable learning environment.
- Building students' self-esteem.

Why is Classroom Management Important?

"Happy, calm children learn best."

- **Daniel Goleman**

The reason why so much emphasis is placed on classroom management in schools is a result of the role it plays in moulding the classroom and the student's experiences. Some of the benefits of classroom management include:

1. **Immense success**

   Proper classroom management drives instructional delivery, which is vital in ensuring students' success in learning as it helps to establish a positive and organised atmosphere that enhances learning by reducing distractions.

2. **Clear behavioural expectations**

   Classroom management helps to set clear behavioural expectations, which, in turn, aids the students in understanding boundaries and the consequences of breaking them. It fosters a respectful and cooperative atmosphere.

3. **Improves teacher's well-being**

   When a classroom is properly managed, energy-sapping situations like stress, noise, and conflicts are minimised, which will enable the teacher to focus more on teaching than managing disruptions and disturbances.

4. **Aids holistic development**

    Excellent classroom management practices support the development of social skills, emotional regulation, and self-discipline among students, thereby guaranteeing holistic development.

5. **Enforces rules and regulations**

    Proper classroom management helps create standard rules and regulations to guide students. Once the teachers create their rules, they can make it clear how erroneous behaviours will be dealt with. Although the recommended model is positive reinforcement and working on good behaviour, there are times when intervening using the rule book is welcomed.

Three Basic Areas of Classroom Management

"If we believe in active student learning, we must consider the variety of ways in which students are encouraged to participate."

-   **Barrie Bennett & Peter Smilanich**

Proper classroom management requires a balance in the three areas of classroom management. These three basic areas are content management, conduct management, and relationship management.

1. **Content management**

   This area focuses on the quality of the teaching and what is being taught in the classroom. It deals more with what is being taught than with who is teaching or learning. It entails how the curriculum and lessons are organised and delivered. It also involves planning lessons, structuring activities, and ensuring that instructional materials are ready and available.

2. **Conduct management**

   This area of classroom management focuses on the behavioural aspect of the classroom and the actions of the students and teachers within it. It focuses on maintaining proper behaviour and discipline within the classroom and also involves establishing clear rules and behavioural expectations. Good conduct management in the classroom helps to address disruptive actions in a timely fashion and also implements suitable sanctions and rewards. A conduct management plan guides the teacher on how to control the classroom and administer consequences. The following are parts of conduct management:

   - Acknowledging responsible behaviour

- Correcting irresponsible behaviour
- Gentle verbal reprimand
- Notification of parents or guardians
- Setting limits outside the classroom

3. **Covenant or relationship management**

   Covenant management is simply building positive relationships between the teacher and students. It sees the classroom group as a social system. The connection between school and community must be constantly revised and modified according to the requirements of societal dynamism. Covenant management encompasses creating a supportive and respectful classroom and addressing the individual needs and interests of the students. Teachers and students relationships are essential to ensuring a positive classroom atmosphere.

Classroom Management Techniques

"The more technique you have, the less you have to worry about it..."

- **Pablo Picasso**

Most educators know how difficult classroom management can be. As essential as it is to the success of the class, which ultimately translates to the success of a school, classroom management is an Achilles' heel for many teachers. Therefore, some techniques will be very helpful. There are many ways to help teachers achieve classroom management, but here are some of the most proven techniques.

1. **Set routines**

   Educators can institute predictable and standardised procedures for beginning and ending classes. A method can also be put in place for the students on how they exit and enter classes, hand in their homework, report disputes and handle materials. By establishing a routine, students know what to do and when to do it, ultimately encouraging good behaviour.

2. **Engage with students actively**

   Before each lesson begins, teachers should engage students by involving them in conversations regarding the learning objectives. This interaction method helps teachers connect closely with students and makes them easier to cooperate with.

3. **Praise and positive reinforcements**

   B.F. Skinner once asserted in an experiment that an animal rewarded for good behaviour will learn much faster and retain what it learns far more effectively than an animal punished for bad behaviour. When students behave exceptionally well, they should be rewarded and acknowledged with praise, incentives, and privileges. This will reinforce such behaviour.

4. **Non-verbal cues**

   When teaching and it is noticed that a student is not paying attention or is trying to disrupt the flow, teachers can employ non-verbal gestures such as finger snapping, eye-rolling, and other cues to gain attention and redirect behaviour without disturbing the teaching flow.

5. **Engaging lessons**

   Lessons should be fun, interesting, and interactive to captivate students' attention and reduce disruptions. Teaching methods that will engage the students actively should be utilised.

Challenges of Classroom Management

"Accept the challenges so you can feel the exhilaration of victory."

   – **George S. Patton**

Implementing classroom management may not always be a smooth process. In the process of implementing it, teachers are always confronted with some challenges, which include, but are not limited to:

1. **Addressing diverse needs**

   One of the biggest challenges of managing a classroom is dealing with the different needs of various students. In a class, there are fast learners and slow learners; consequently, when teachers try to tailor their teaching to suit the fast learners, the slow ones find it difficult to catch up. Hence, teachers have to adopt different teaching modes that are suitable for the entire class.

2. **Poor knowledge of students**

   It is recommended that teachers possess relevant knowledge about their students. However, it is quite challenging for them to have the necessary knowledge about all their students. Nevertheless, good teachers try their best to understand the abilities, personalities, interests, backgrounds, and triggers of each student. Without this knowledge, teachers will have a difficult time giving instructions and setting up measures that can keep each student organised.

3. **Overwhelming class size**

   Managing a class of 10 students cannot be the same as managing a class of 50 or 100. It takes a lot to hold the attention of a large class because the larger the class, the greater the distractions.

4. **Insufficient knowledge of subjects**

    When teachers are asked to teach subjects they have an insufficient understanding of, it becomes a recipe for a disorganised classroom. The teacher will be unable to relay the lessons in the subject, which will give rise to many questions from the students. In cases where teachers have no direct answers, they resort to scolding and threatening the students not to ask questions. All these breeds a disorganised and dishevelled classroom.

5. **Shoddy learning environment**

    When the learning space is not conducive or is open to many distractions, managing the class becomes difficult. So, right from the inception of designing a school and classrooms, the teachers and students should be considered, not just the aesthetics. If there are too many distractions around, teachers will have a hard time getting the students' attention.

4

BEHAVIOURAL MANAGEMENT AND POSITIVE DISCIPLINE

Jim Rohn once said, "Discipline is the bridge between goals and accomplishments". For students, the teachers are the ones who help them bridge the gap between the goals at the beginning of the term and their accomplishments at the end of it. Consequently, if we go by Jim Rohn's assertions, we cannot metamorphose from one point to another without discipline. As a result, discipline remains one of the best ways teachers can make their classroom a haven for their students and foster inclusiveness.

What is Positive Discipline?

Positive discipline is a classroom management programme that uses respectful communication, problem-solving, and reinforcement of good behaviour rather than punitive measures to teach. Positive discipline can also be used by parents to communicate what behaviours are acceptable, which ones are not, the rewards of behaving well, and the consequences of not. The positive discipline approach involves setting clear expectations, using consistent rules, praise and rewards, and helping students understand the consequences of their actions, which will lead to improved student behaviour, higher self-esteem, and a positive classroom atmosphere.

The Differences between Punishment and Positive Discipline

Punishment and positive discipline should not be mistaken for the same thing because the definitions are simple and varied. Punishment is a penalty imposed on a student for their misdemeanours, while, on the other hand, positive discipline is the act of training or teaching a student how to obey rules. They both use different methods. Below are the differences between the two:

S/N	Punishment	Positive Discipline
1	Verbal	Praise
2	disapproval	Rewards
3	Reprimands	Positive remarks
4	Emotional abuse	Problem-solving
5	Physical abuse	Respect
	Starvation	

Principles of Behavioural Management

"Too often we forget that discipline really means to teach, not to punish."

- **Dr. Daniel Siegel and Tina Payne Bryson** (The Whole-Brain Child")

Here are some of the principles that guide behavioural management:

Principle 1: Behaviour is largely a product of its immediate environment

Some people believe that the environment has more effect on us than even how we were trained. Sometimes, it is hard to dispute this. As a result, when a child or student begins to exhibit unwholesome behaviours, parents and teachers often either change the environment or remove the child totally from it.

Key: *Sound teachers provide and foster a fun and safe environment so they can monitor their students.*

Principle 2: Behaviour is shaped by consequences

There are two major consequences that shape children's behaviour and teach them accountability and responsibility. They are natural and logical consequences. Natural consequences occur normally as a result of children's behaviour, while logical consequences are interventions teachers or parents use to facilitate change. For example, if a child refuses to study, it is natural for him or her to fail the course (natural consequence). On the other hand, if a student is being disruptive, a logical consequence might be moving their seat to minimise distractions for both the student and others.

Key: *Natural and logical consequences should be used wisely to shape healthy behaviours.*

Principle 3: Behaviour is ultimately shaped better by positive rather than negative consequence

As stated earlier, the famous psychologist, B.F Skinner, affirmed that rewards tend to motivate good behavioural dispositions much more than punishments do. Therefore, the key is for teachers to discover the rewards that most motivate each student. For some, the most motivating reward may be a sticker or being granted extra reading or recess time. However, for many children, receiving approval and encouragement from their parents and teachers remain their most potent reward. If a child raises his or her hand to ask a question and the teacher praises that polite behaviour, the child will be more likely to raise his or her hand the next time the teacher asks a question because the behaviour was followed by a desirable outcome; the preceding action is strengthened.

Key: *Positive reinforcement should be applied often to guide children's behaviour.*

Principle 4: Past behaviour is the best predictor of future behaviour.

If certain previous behaviours occur repeatedly, skilled parents and teachers understand that the behaviour is likely to occur again. Thus, taking advantage of SLOs (Student Learning Objectives) is important so children can learn that certain behaviours come with both desired and undesired consequences. As a result, children will learn which behaviours are appropriate and which are inappropriate.

Key: *Past and present behaviours should be carefully monitored to facilitate appropriate consequences to address future behaviours.*

Strategies for Promoting Good Behaviour

To promote good behaviour among students and create a good learning environment for all, here are some verified strategies:

Strategy 1: Verbally acknowledge appropriate behaviour in a positive way.

Good behaviour, if rewarded through encouragement or praise, tends to motivate children to exhibit other positive and appropriate behaviours because children like to please others and, as a natural consequence, to feel good about themselves. Therefore, reward desired behaviours with praise.

Strategy 2: Acknowledge appropriate behaviour intermittently.

One proven way to promote a specific positive behaviour is to acknowledge it almost every time it happens. Once the behaviour occurs, a proven strategy is to acknowledge it the first time, then the second time, and so on, until the behaviour becomes permanent (Skinner, 1938). After the behaviour is firmly established, rewarding it occasionally is normally enough to sustain it.

Strategy 3: Acknowledge appropriate behaviour casually and briefly.

Acknowledging appropriate behaviour briefly and casually lets children and students know that their positive behaviours are noticed and that it is the expected norm. If teachers and parents fawn over children and exaggerate "how great" their positive behaviours are, they may come to depend on them too much for positive affirmations or somehow rationalise that they deserve continued and increased praise for simply doing what is expected as normal behaviour.

Strategy 4: Give variety to verbal praise.

Giving variety to verbal praise helps a child distinguish between the types of behaviours that are being noticed, and it also helps teachers avoid redundancy. Below are some examples of at least four types of variety that can be used when providing verbal praise.

Descriptive praise: "You stacked the blocks so carefully, one on top of the other. What are you making?"

Deserved praise: "I appreciate your being so nice to your classmates".

Sincere praise: "I can tell your parents like it when you excel in your studies".

Values-rich praise: "I am proud of you for telling the truth".

Strategy 5: Communicate to children and students that they are lovable and capable.

Parents and teachers need to focus on sending children two primary messages: (1) they are lovable and (2) they are capable (Coplen & MacArthur, 1982). Teachers can show children they are lovable by being warm, connecting with them, and monitoring and paying attention to their behaviours so they know they are cared for. They can help children feel capable by creating situations that require them to solve problems on their own, therefore giving them competency experiences for growth and development, and by providing multiple opportunities for children to engage in all types of learning. However, attempting to dominate children by exerting power and control over them or by trying to overprotect them by not allowing them to learn from their mistakes will strike out against their feelings of capability.

The Five Positive Methods of Discipline in the Classroom

There is a saying, "Teach a child the way he should go". Children learn better when taught gently than when forced, and they assimilate better when positively disciplined compared to when punished. Some teachers tend to prefer punitive measures over positive discipline; this should not be so. By using positive discipline techniques like redirection, praise, and selective ignoring, bad behaviour can be nipped in the bud without resorting to threats, yelling, or physical punishment. Proponents of positive discipline claim that the method helps strengthen bonds and increases trust between parents and children. When adults respond to provocation from children with the five tried-and-true methods of positive discipline instead of anger, they teach the children that it is possible to respond to frustrating moments without conflict.

Methods of Positive Discipline

1. **Token reinforcement**

   In token reinforcement, points or tokens are awarded to a student for good behaviour. The rewards themselves have little to no value, but they can be exchanged for something valuable. For example, if a student answers questions correctly in class, the teacher could give them a ticket that can be exchanged for a prize at the end of the week or term.

2. **Tangible reinforcement**

   These refer to toys, stickers, awards, and balloons given to kids when they exhibit good behaviour. However, in some cases, handing out tangible gifts may make other students envious. If that is the case, or depending on what the school permits, awards, certificates, or written notes to the parents eulogising a student's progress could be used.

3. **Social reinforcement**

   This is an expression of approval and praise for appropriate behaviour. These expressions can come in three different forms: verbal, written, and other physical expressions.

   - Verbal is the use of words and comments like "well done", "good job", "you've done great", "I'm proud of you", and many others.

   - Written approval includes letters and remarks on their books, for example, excellent on a completed worksheet.

   - Other physical expressions could be a thumbs-up, a bright smile, or a nod.

4. **Activity reinforcement**

This method involves permitting students to take part in their preferred activities when they behave well. For example, if they pass their tests, they can be allowed to participate in the next big school activity.

5. **Direct reinforcement**

   Direct reinforcement refers to a teaching process in which the teacher influences a student's behaviour through the consequences of their actions. If a behaviour is followed by a positive consequence (reward), the student is more likely to repeat the behaviour. Conversely, if a behaviour is followed by a negative consequence (a reprimand), the student is less likely to repeat it. Direct reinforcement simply means students' behaviours are shaped through the use of positive or negative consequences.

5

INSTRUCTIONS THAT WORK

Instructions are like rules that guide or a compass that points the way to go so that one does not get lost. Instruction is vital in education, as it is the transfer of learning from one person to another. If narrowed down to the classroom, it is the passing down of information from the teacher to the students. Instruction is the creation and implementation of purpose-driven plans for guiding the process through which learners gain knowledge and understanding and develop skills, attitudes, and values. Instruction is frequently associated with the term "curriculum" and generally refers to the teaching methods and learning activities that a teacher uses to deliver the curriculum in the classroom. The terms "teaching" and "instruction" are often used interchangeably. (Kridel, 2010).

Modern Teaching Methods that Work

"In teaching, it is the method and not the content that is the message."

- **Ashley Montagu**

There is a shift from traditional teaching methods to modern ones, and the effects of modern teaching methods on students have been impressive. The traditional method is a teacher-centric one that promotes the supremacy of the teachers within the classroom and focuses on them as the sole source of knowledge and information within the classroom. Students taught with this method learn through repetition and memorisation. On the other hand, modern teaching methods integrate more activity-based techniques that focus on student learning via new and innovative ideas rather than making them recite the syllabus. In modern teaching methods, curriculum teaching and planning are customised to meet the specific needs of the learners. These methods help the students actively participate to build their knowledge and sharpen their skills.

There are various modern teaching methods educators can imbibe, and they include:

1. **Flipped classroom**

   This is also called reversed learning. The main objective of this instruction method is to optimise time in class. A flipped classroom is the most popular modern teaching method today. In the traditional method, students are introduced to a topic first by their teacher and then study more about it on their own at home. However, in a flipped classroom, students will first learn about the topic independently at home, and then they will come to the classroom with questions.

2. **Project-based learning**

   This allows students to acquire knowledge and skills through the development of projects that solve real-life problems. In this learning method, the teacher assigns a practical or theoretical project, and students work to materialise the project. Teachers can assign these projects to them individually or as a group, and the objectives must be to provide solutions to practical life issues, not abstract ones. The projects the teacher assigns should be:
   - Hands-on
   - Collaborative
   - Multidisciplinary
   - Student-centred
   - Real-time
   - Real-life based
   - Flexible

3. **Cooperative learning**

   Cooperative learning is a teaching method where teachers assign students to work together in small groups to achieve a common goal or complete a task.

It often involves collaborative activities such as group discussions, projects, and peer teaching that enable students to share knowledge. Cooperative learning can enhance problem-solving skills, communication abilities, and overall learning outcomes. The final goal is usually achieved if each member successfully performs assigned tasks.

4. **Gamification**

    When educators employ the use of game design elements, mechanics, and principles in non-game contexts to engage and teach students, it is called "gamification". This modern teaching technique typically includes elements like points, badges, leaderboards, challenges, and rewards to encourage participation and achievement.

5. **Problem-based learning**

    Problem-based learning (PBL) is an instructional approach where students learn by actively engaging with real-world problems or scenarios. PBL focuses on posing open-ended, complex problems to students and guiding them through a process of investigation, research, and problem-solving. It also helps students develop critical thinking and problem-solving skills, and a deeper understanding of the subject matter.

6. **VAK learning**

   VAK learning is broader than the other methods as it is well suited for three different types of learners: visual, auditory, and kinaesthetic. Visual learners absorb information better when they view the material (textbooks, presentations, infographics, diagrams, charts, etc.). Auditory learners retain content better when they hear it (podcasts, videos, discussions), and kinaesthetic learners learn better when they act out the content. VAK learning has something for everyone. By using different types of learning materials, it is possible to identify with greater accuracy the individual problems of each student.

7. **Thinking-based learning**

   Thinking-based learning can (and should) be combined with all teaching styles as it is a complementary type of learning. A thinking-based activity involves asking deeper questions and challenging the truth of a given fact. Thinking-based learning can also come in the form of self-reflection after completing a project. The teacher prompts learners to identify what went right and what went wrong in their approach and what they could have done instead. This teaching strategy enhances critical thinking, analytical thinking skills, and self-awareness.

8. **Competency-based learning**

    Competency-based learning can also be used with other methods. In competency-based learning, teachers use learners' assessments and hands-on projects to confirm if the learner has achieved the desired learning objectives and is fit to move on to a more advanced level of learning. Competency-based learning is, by default, personalised. The course curriculum is not predetermined; it is continuously adjusted depending on the student's performance.

Advantages of Modern Teaching Methods

1. **Engagement**

    Modern teaching methods make learning more interactive and engaging for students through the use of technology, multimedia, and hands-on activities. It teaches them in a language and manner they will understand.

2. **Personalisation**

    Modern methods of teaching allow for personalised learning experiences as they cater to individual student's needs and adjust to their learning styles. It identifies each student's strengths and weaknesses and develops the best teaching method that suits them.

3. **Accessibility**

Modern methods of teaching incorporate technology, and technology-based methods provide access to a wide range of educational resources and opportunities, breaking down environmental barriers. When technology is used, it transcends immediate geographical location. As a result of technology, students can now access any educational material they desire from anywhere.

4. **Collaboration**

Unlike the traditional method, which is teacher-centric and requires students to be focused on their educators, modern teaching methods foster collaboration among students, which, in turn, encourages teamwork and better communication skills, which are imperative soft skills needed for future endeavours.

5. **Real-world relevance**

In traditional methods of teaching, there was the challenge of practicality, as lessons were mostly abstract. However, many modern methods focus on real-world applications, helping students apply what they learn to practical situations.

6. **Data-driven insights**

Technology enables the collection and analysis of data on students' performances, helping teachers fine-tune their instruction for better results. Thus, it is easier to keep track of all students' performance, know their strengths and weaknesses, and provide teaching methods that will suit their peculiarities.

7. **Flexibility**

Modern methods often allow for flexible learning schedules, accommodating diverse student needs and lifestyles.

8. **Skill development**

These modern teaching methods help push the students to reach their potential and bring out their innate abilities because they emphasise critical thinking, problem-solving, and digital literacy skills, thereby preparing them for the demands of the 21st century.

9. **Continuous learning**

Online resources and tools facilitate lifelong learning and professional development for both students and educators.

10. **Inclusion**

Modern teaching methods accommodate students with disabilities, ensuring a more inclusive learning environment. Overall, modern teaching methods aim to enhance the quality of education by adapting to the evolving needs of students and society.

6
PROFESSIONALISM IN SCHOOL

Professionalism refers to the set of behaviours, qualities, and standards that are expected in a particular occupation, industry, or workplace. It involves acting in a responsible, ethical, and competent manner while adhering to the norms and values of a given profession. Professionalism often includes qualities like integrity, reliability, punctuality, courtesy, and a commitment to continuous improvement in one's skills and knowledge. It is essential for building trust and maintaining a positive reputation in the professional world.

Professionalism involves consistently achieving high standards, both visibly and "behind the scenes", irrespective of your role or profession. "Fitting in" is a big part of professionalism, as it is a way of showing respect, attention to detail, and a commitment to upholding agreed practices and values. However, being true to oneself is just as important. True professionals do not follow rules mindlessly; they know when and how to challenge the norms. They are also flexible and find their own ways to do things while still maintaining high standards.

What is Professional Behaviour in School?

"The life you live is the lesson you teach"

- **Unknown**

Professional behaviour in school is a combination of the teacher's attitude, appearance, teaching methods, and manners. The main principles of professional work behaviour for a teacher include:

- Treating managers, colleagues, and students with respect
- Projecting a positive attitude
- Being polite
- Showing good judgement
- Being ethical
- Dressing properly

    Teachers who show professionalism at work are often productive, motivated, and perform at a high level.

Characteristics of Professionalism

There are certain characteristics that teachers who uphold professionalism should embody. There are:

- **Competence**

    A professional always gets the job done well. When the abilities of an individual match the requirements of their job description, the results produced will often exceed expectations. A professional does not just put-up appearances for the sake of higher authority but displays a high level of competence, which would be evident in his or her output. For a professional teacher, competency reveals itself in how well the class is managed, how teaching methods are adjusted to suit each student's learning style, how effectively student learning is tracked, etc. If a teacher is unable to achieve these, he or she is not competent.

- **Knowledge**

  Professionalism involves updating one's knowledge bank regularly. The world is evolving and new concepts are being introduced into every discipline. It is necessary for teachers to keep improving on what they know and be abreast of the latest developments in the teaching field. At every stage of one's career, it is important to master one's role and to keep adding to what one knows to avoid being outdated. It is also important that teachers put their knowledge to practical use when required. Being confident enough to put this newly acquired knowledge to help others succeed and to solve problems is a vital aspect of professionalism.

- **Integrity**

Integrity is a core principle of professionals. Professionals are honest. They do not compromise their values even in tough situations, because they understand work ethics.

- **Emotional intelligence**

  To be a true professional, it is imperative to stay professional even under pressure. This includes developing strategies to manage emotions and having a clear awareness of other people's feelings. Possessing emotional intelligence is very important. Emotional intelligence enables a teacher to know when and how to express some concerns. A teacher with a high level of emotional intelligence will know how to handle conflicts in the classroom as well as conflicts outside the classroom.

- **Appropriateness**

  A huge part of being professional is knowing and doing what is right in different situations. It eliminates awkwardness, boosts credibility, and helps the teacher feel secure in his or her role. Appropriateness is revealed in outward appearances such as dressing, personal grooming, and body language. It also covers the way a teacher speaks and writes, the topics he or she chooses to discuss, and his or her attitude towards others.

- **Respect**

  Professionalism means being a role model for good manners and being polite to everyone, not just those who are in charge of the pay check or in authority. Respect is truly expressed when the needs of others who have nothing to offer are taken into consideration and their rights are upheld as humans who deserve love and kindness.

Effects of Lack of Professionalism in School

When professionalism is poor or lacking in a school, a lot can go wrong. The standard of a school will be ruined when the teachers in that school behave unprofessionally. Below are some of the effects of having unprofessional teachers:

1. **Wrong attire**

   When teachers are not professional, they wear clothing that does not align with the school's dress code. They could also dress indecently by wearing revealing or overtly tight-fitting clothes, which could cause major teaching distractions. Unprofessional teachers groom themselves poorly and often appear shabby, therefore giving the school a bad image.

2. **Lateness**

Punctuality is the soul of business. Good time management is a skill every professional should have. Teachers are role models to the students they teach, and when they do not uphold a certain value, it becomes difficult to demand it from the students. Consistently arriving late to work or meetings without a valid reason is disrespectful, unprofessional, and can affect students' performance.

3. **Poor Communication**

   A teacher's major job is communication; so, failing to communicate clearly and professionally through emails, phone calls, or in-person interactions can lead to misunderstandings and conflicts. Teachers should learn how to communicate correctly with colleagues, superiors, and students. It is unprofessional to communicate in ways that will send the wrong message or that will not deliver the message at all.

4. **Disregard for policies**

   Ignoring or breaking company policies and rules demonstrates a lack of respect for the organisation and its values. Teachers who lack the right degree of professionalism constantly disregard the policies put in place by the school to guide their conduct. When these teachers disregard the school authorities, it makes it difficult for their students to obey regulations, as children are sometimes very sensitive and observant about their environment.

5. **Offensive language**

Unprofessional teachers use offensive or disrespectful language in conversation or written communication. They use such language when speaking to their students, superiors, and colleagues, thereby creating a toxic and inhumane learning environment.

6. **Neglecting responsibilities**

When a school has unprofessional staff, responsibilities are often neglected because no one cares about obeying the rules. Tasks will not be completed, deadlines will not be met, the curriculum and accepted teaching methods will not be used to teach the students, etc. All these harm the school's dynamics and outlook.

7. **Disruptive behaviour**

This manifests in teachers displaying disruptive or disrespectful manners during meetings, presentations, or in shared workspaces, which can create a hostile work environment. Unprofessional teachers interrupt meetings rudely and generally conduct themselves poorly in school.

8. **Lack of ethical behaviour**

Unethical practices, such as dishonesty, fraud, or conflicts of interest, reflect a severe lack of professionalism.

How to Maintain Professionalism in School

To maintain professional behaviour among staff in a school, there are some principles and habits that should be emphasised. There are:

1. **Right dressing**: Staff should be encouraged to follow the dress code of the school.
2. **Punctuality**: Arriving on time for work and to the class for teaching should be made compulsory.
3. **Good communication**: The importance of using clear and respectful communication with colleagues, supervisors, and students should be stressed.
4. **Integrity**: Teachers should act with honesty and transparency in all their dealings. Unethical behaviour such as lying or cheating should be discouraged.
5. **Conflict resolution**: Conflicts should be addressed professionally and constructively, seeking resolution rather than escalating issues.

6. **Time management**: Tasks should be prioritised. Time should also be managed efficiently to maximise productivity.

7. **Social media**: Comments and posts made on social media should not be done in a way that can ruin professional image.

8. **Respect for diversity**: Everyone, regardless of their background, beliefs, or roles in the school, should be treated with respect.

9. **Teamwork**: Teachers should collaborate and not compete. Team spirit can be built with collaboration.

10. **Problem-solving**: Challenges should be tackled with a constructive mind-set that seeks solutions rather than dwelling on the problems.

11. **Adaptability**: Being open to change and willing to learn new skills or technologies will boost professionalism.

12. **Feedback**: Feedback from supervisors and colleagues is an opportunity for growth and improvement.

13. **Professional development**: Trainings, workshops, and skill-building opportunities can be held to aid staff in their professional development.

14. **Etiquette**: Proper etiquette, whether in person or virtually, should be adhered to.

Demonstrating professional behaviour does not only contribute to a positive work environment but also enhances reputation and increases long-term career prospects.

7

PLANNING INSTRUCTION

One of the most important responsibilities of a teacher is the planning of instruction, especially at the commencement of a session. Planning instruction provides direction and assessment guidelines and conveys instructional intent to students and supervisors. It is one of the six imperative skills all teachers must possess. Instructional planning is a process where the teacher uses the right curriculum, instructional strategies, resources, and data during the planning process to address the diverse needs of students.

Modern teachers use instructional planning as a tool to design what topics or objectives students will learn at the beginning of every session and how they will get them to learn these topics. Good instructional planning should include:

- Specific objectives students should achieve.
- Short-term and long-term goals.
- Support that will be provided by teachers.
- Methods that students will engage in to reach these goals including individual and group activities.
- Research and data to show how activities will help students reach their goals.
- Assessments that teachers will use to monitor individual performance.
- Material that will be needed, including primary and supplementary material.

Importance of Instructional Planning

Instructional planning is important because:

- Good planning is the first step to effective instructional delivery
- A well-planned class reduces stress for the teacher and helps minimise disruptions.
- When students are engaged during the entire class period, they have less opportunity to cause disruptions.
- The teacher's demeanour, lesson plan quality, and method of delivery all contribute to a productive day in class.

Basic Components of Instructional Planning

The components of instructional planning include:

- Creating goals
- Choosing methodologies and strategies
- Selecting relevant assessments

One of the most crucial parts of instructional planning is deciding on specific educational objectives that the students will be expected to achieve.

Steps for Planning Instructions

Before beginning instructional planning, teachers should look into texts and supplemental materials to determine what concepts they must cover from the beginning of the session to the end. Here are specific steps to take when planning instruction:

- Create detailed unit lesson plans, which should include objectives, activities, time estimates, and required materials.
- Plan the timeline.
- Create assessments, including classwork, homework, and tests.
- Write a daily lesson outline and agenda. The teacher should have an agenda prepared for herself and her students so that he or she is organised and retains students' interest. The teacher can lose students' attention if he or she has to search for a page to read or has to fumble through a stack of papers.
- Create and/or gather the required items ahead of time. This can include making hand-outs, movies, lecture notes, or manipulatives (learning objects, such as pennies for counting). Teachers should always plan ahead.
- Plan for the unexpected. Interruptions and unexpected events often occur in class. Teachers should prepare for these.

- Create mini-lessons to help fill up any time that might be left at the end of a class period. Even the best teachers are sometimes left with extra time.

Importance of Instructional Planning

Instructional planning is crucial in education for several reasons:

1. **Alignment with learning Goals**

   Instructional planning ensures that teaching activities, materials, and assessments align with the intended learning objectives. This alignment increases the likelihood that students will achieve desired outcomes. It also makes it easy for the teacher to measure the success of the lesson.

2. **Engagement and motivation**

   Thoughtful planning can incorporate engaging and motivating activities that capture students' interest, making the learning experience more enjoyable.

3. **Differentiation**

   Planning allows educators to tailor instruction to meet the diverse needs of students. It enables the inclusion of strategies and resources for students with varied abilities, learning styles, and backgrounds.

4. **Assessment and feedback**

Planning includes designing assessments that measure students' progress accurately. It also allows for the timely provision of feedback, which is essential for student improvement.

5. **Time management**

Planning ensures that instructional time is used efficiently. Teachers can allocate time for various activities, ensuring that important concepts are covered to avoid rushed or skipped content.

6. **Resource allocation**

It helps educators identify the resources they will need during instruction, such as textbooks, technology, or manipulatives, and ensures these resources are available.

7. **Professional development**

Collaborative planning among educators promotes the sharing of best practices and professional growth, ultimately benefiting both teachers and students.

8. **Adaptation to changing needs**

Planning allows for flexibility. Educators can adjust their plans based on ongoing assessment data and student feedback, making sure that instruction remains responsive to changing needs.

9. **Long-term goals**

It helps educators consider the long-term progression of learning, guaranteeing that each lesson fits into a broader curriculum and prepares students for future content.

10. Accountability

Instructional planning can provide a clear framework for evaluating teaching performance and programme effectiveness, aiding in accountability measures.

All in all, instructional planning is the backbone of effective teaching. It maximises the potential for student learning by ensuring that instruction is purposeful, organised, and adaptable to the needs of learners.

Instructional Planning Strategies

There are many verified strategies or methods teachers can use while designing their instruction. One strategy is backward planning. By using backward planning, teachers can create a strategic plan to help guide their lessons. Before instruction, they may begin planning by asking what the objectives or goals for the unit will be. To do this, some questions they should ask are:

- What do I want my students to learn?
- What do my students need to know before moving on to the next unit?

- What are my students struggling with, based on past assessments?
- What are my students' strengths, based on past assessments?
- What challenges might my students face during this unit?
- How can I prepare my students to reach these goals?

To help guide their initial planning, teachers can decide on the essential questions they want their students to answer by the end of the unit. These questions must be intentional and specific. Essential questions aid in formulating learning objectives in a way that can enable students to think critically about them.

During instructional planning, teachers should think about how they can adapt their instruction based on their observations. After the instruction is complete, teachers must reflect on their instruction delivery to create informed plans for the future. They should ask:

- How did my students respond to this activity?
- How can I help students who are struggling with this concept?
- How do I deal with students who are achieving faster than expected?

REFERENCES

Coplen, R. D., & MacArthur, J. D. (1982). *Developing a healthy self-image*. Provo, UT: Brigham Young University Press.

Fernandez, AC, Huang, J., and Ronaldo, V. (2011). "Does where a student sit really matter?–The impact of seating locations on student classroom learning". *International Journal of Applied Educational Studies*, 10(1).

https://study.com/learn/lesson/instructional-planning-quality-materials-strategies-examples.html

https://www.bookwidgets.com/blog/2019/12/19-classroom-seating-arrangements-fit-for-your-teaching

https://www.thoughtco.com/planning-and-organizing-instruction-8391

https://www.verywellfamily.com/concerns-about-giving-kids-rewards-1094886

https://www.verywellfamily.com/facts-about-corporal-punishment-1094806

https://www.verywellfamily.com/types-of-child-discipline-1095064

M. K. Nambiar, Radha; Mohd Noor, Noorizah; Ismail, Kemboja (2018). "The impact of new learning spaces on teacher pedagogy and student learning behavior". *INTED2018 Proceedings*. Vol. 1. pp. 8132–8135. doi:10.21125/inted.2018.1969. ISBN 978-84-697-9480-7.

McCorskey, James C.; McVetta, Rod W. (1978-03-01). "Classroom seating arrangements: Instructional communication theory versus student preferences". *Communication Education*. 27 (2): 99–111. Doi: 10.1080/03634527809378281. ISSN 0363-4523.

Strategies for Promoting Good Behaviour

The Five Positive Methods of Discipline in the Classroom

Methods of Positive Discipline

5. INSTRUCTIONS THAT WORK

Modern Teaching Methods that Work

Advantages of Modern Teaching Methods

6. PROFESSIONALISM IN THE SCHOOL

What is Professional Behaviour in the School?

Characteristics of Professionalism

Effects of Lack of Professionalism in the School

How to Maintain Professionalism in the School

7. PLANNING INSTRUCTIONS

Importance of Instructional Planning

Basic Components of Instructional Planning

Steps for Planning Instructions

Importance of Instructional Planning

Instructional Planning Strategies